AUDACITY

TO SPEAK OUT LOUD

PRIYANKA SHEKHAR

ISBN 979-888521864-1

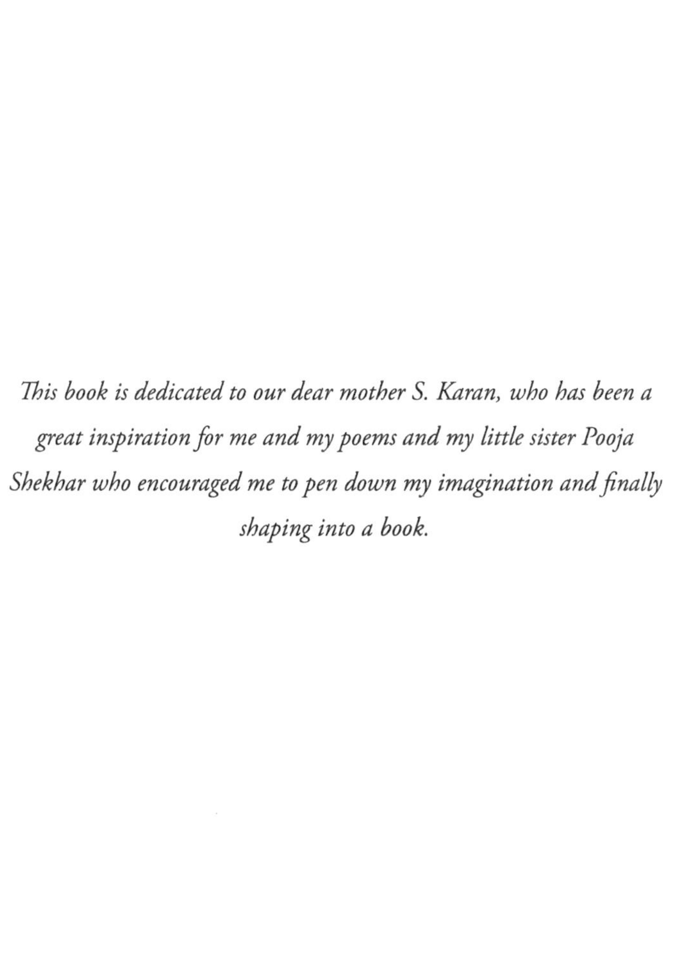

This book is dedicated to our dear mother S. Karan, who has been a great inspiration for me and my poems and my little sister Pooja Shekhar who encouraged me to pen down my imagination and finally shaping into a book.

Contents

Foreword

The book Audacity is a collection of poems with strong emotions coming up bold to the touch of love, compassion, patriotism, and togetherness. These poems cherish and celebrate humanity and the presence of relationships that becomes the strength for survival. The poems are the connecting dots of a person to another person, accepting them, rejecting them using an audacious tone.

The author has tried to show all the possible colours of life within and out as per the perception of humans towards the beauty and the struggles in the world. At the same time, the author seems to be inspired by the hard work people are putting in and is highly grateful for having been born in this world.

Preface

Some of the poems in this book has been inspired by real incidences in my life and a few are the flight of imagination. Nonetheless in both cases it is way too satisfying as the ideas never disappointed my imagination. To my surprise, it was more promising than I ever expected.

The closest to my heart is 'The Mother of Thy' which is dedicated to my mother and all the mothers in the globe and 'The Butterfly of My Life' which is dedicated to my sister whose sweet and innocent behaviour brought the light of hope and happiness in my life. And what inspired me the most is the contribution of farmers and soldiers who work rigorously day and night towards the society to fulfil their duties which we sometimes fail to acknowledge. They are the most essential role in society, towards satiating our hunger as well as letting us sleep in peace.

Acknowledgements

To the beautiful world which contributed their energies towards the making of this book and a fine me who is able to deliver you a beautiful melody of rhythmic as well as non-rhythmic pieces of life's phases, relationships and duties. I am grateful to all those who inspired me to bring forth these diverse ideas into a single book. I would also like to acknowledge my mother who has been a great inspiration for my poems who stood by my side all along giving me strength, encouragement.

Secondly, I would like to thank my sister who has always been there guiding and supporting me throughout the journey of making this book a reality for me, none the less she put in all her time and dedication towards the editing of this book.

Thirdly, I would like to convey my gratitude towards my publisher for providing me with a platform to reach out to people and publish my work. At last but not least, I would like to thank all mighty who has provided my pen with the grace to be able to produce such fragments of human lives with all his blessings into words and create poetry.

Prologue

Desire

Have you ever heard about the satiated desire
It's nothing but to put everyone else on fire
To exhaust ourselves, the weak and tire
To impress the inner self, to agonise with ire
There could be times when consequences are dire
Though we choose greed, to be a perfect liar
In the name of necessity and all we require
It's not a compulsion, we want to move shire
To release the luxury, all services hire
Though we can live comfortably, we dig up mire
It's hard work that is needed to be sapphire
Instead of an easy way, we choose haywire
Life is too tough, not when we live
Life is too rough, not when we struggle
It becomes a true challenge when one aspires
When we desire, things are set up on fire
At last, it is taught by life
'Whatever you receive, respect and admire'

Priyanka Shekhar

1. The Mother Of Thy

The arms holding you tight
With all her love and might
Don't forget o'heart,
It was hers
Who did not let you off her sight,
When you were innocent, ignorant a child of eight
Don't forget o'heart,
That hand to hold you, it was hers
When your speech was not even right
When you were wounded in a neighbourhood fight
The soothing touch on your soul comforting
Don't forget o'heart it was hers
When you could barely manage alright
The struggle with world knackered you outright
The one to hold you in her lap to let you lose your cries
Don't forget o'heart it was her
It was in a wink of an eye the days changed,
The gloomy darkness of the night brought a beautiful warm sunlight
So it's your journey on a golden path alone
Did you forget her fairy sight?
When the dusk brought anew and bright

A day of hope and promising sunlight
A soothing breeze and calm moonlight
The mayhem is no longer for you to be fright
O'heart did forget her fairy sight?
Once success knocked the maiden's door
Your heart is regretful and abhor
Do you not remember that heaven's shore?
Which uplifted you from your lowly plight?
O'heart did you forget her fairy sight?
O'heavens, O'god, a day will come
When water retreats and fate takes turn
The beauty and valour be lost in time
Only one shadow cool will save your cries
She won't forget you the mother of thy

2. Filial Child

I am afraid to express my dreams, my ambitions
Will I ever get to pursue my deep-rooted passion?
It's for me to explore the world as I see it
There is nothing like I am giving up on my responsibilities
Will you choose to let loose and give me permission?
For it's what I really want, not mere obsession
The hurtful image of being able to fly
As the wings have grown but unable to try
Will I receive a sense of security, comprehension?
Or will you remain thinking of me as a precious possession?
Let me try my own calibre,
I am not only testing the waters
I yearn to sail on foreign land
Under the dreaded moon and the dreary sand
Don't pamper and tie me strings
Let me loose, give me wings
I would go far, won't go wild
I won't ever leave you
I am your filial child

3. Let Thy Imagination Fly

Let thy imagination fly high in the sky
Despite being hidden under the clouds
Let the bright light of sunshine with all its might
Break with the dim ray of dawn
Let the ray of hope a better future be shown
Hold the hands of opportunity to be
Eliminate the dearth of thy misery
No hidden gem can be polished without a try
No aspiration can take a leap and bound to fly
Until there is a base of broken heart and dreams
Let the fragments make a masterpiece of your life
Once you take a baby step
Don't be afraid of the stones and the bumps ahead
It is there to turn your potential to the fullest
To test you through and make you refine
Let the test be taken
Let hardships show
Once the wings are broken, they can always re-grow
With all your might you try
Do not be ashamed of or be shy
Your skill will never go in vain
There is a rainbow after each rain

Let nature be the witness of your struggle
Don't be afraid let it flow
Let thy imaginations eliminate all your trouble
Be broken but be beautiful
Be shaken but be dutiful
Start from the dust and touch the sky
Let thy imagination fly high

4. Birdie

I knew no boundaries when I was born
I am a free bird in the world is all I've known
I opened my eyes and saw my mother
Holding me beneath her lovely feather
She patted my back and fed me food
She kept me from evil, showed the good
She didn't leave me off her sight
Never let me participate in a birdie's fight
She brought me up with utmost care
For her, I was the only dear
She raised me day, she raised me night
While guarding me with all her might
One day I asked her,
When will I fly?
When will you let loose?
When will I try?
That day she couldn't sleep a wink
She fell sick as withered all her mink
Deep down she worried and heavily sighed
My boy, this world is not just alright
I can't leave you be yourself in the blue sky
For you, there is waiting humongous tide

Don't go out and about the world
You are unaware of how things will turn
I didn't like her nagging
Decided and took a flee
Enjoyed a lot
Cared less
Went free
Faced the sudden misery
That was the beginning
My bad day
Man was hunter
and
I was prey
Thank god! His preference was 'Veg'!
He caught me and sold me in the cage.

5. Nasty Scar

The smile on her face, all bright and shiny
Shadowed the reflection of night gloomy
Woke up fresh, charged on fired
Not even a sign of feeling tired
Iron lady for her kids so far
She has always acted as a strengthened spar
Didn't let her ship tumble in the tide
However, she struggled she had to hide
Smiled from ear to ear to make kids laugh
Was respected among her secretarial staff
Fought her fight with all her strength
Never begged for help
For it was not she couldn't rely
Back in the date, she too had tried
She trusted but got stabbed
Received jealousy and hatred in her sack
For she, couldn't think who she had wronged
How relations turned back and things went wrong
She was treated a mere 'golden egg-laying hen'
To mischief her, simplicity and innocence everyone feigns
She could recognise but couldn't take revenge
As her nature was totally strange

For her children to grow well she endured pain
Didn't talk back and struggled again
She has lived her life mediocre and come so far
Along with a nasty scar.

6. Sister's Grief

What if she is firstborn?
What if I am second?
Why don't I get the first say?
Am I less important?
Is it advantageous being born first?
For the second is disadvantageous
Why can she be all rude and rough?
And I am expected to behave courteous?
Is it my fault or society is to blame?
What have I done ever to always endure the pain?
Why is she opinionated?
And I mute?
Aren't both siblings?
For only me, why the world so brute?
I am expected patience while being at loss
Why she gets to win every toss?
Why I grow calmer, when she still acts a child?
Why she can express her anger?
And I ought to be mild?
Isn't the irony of situation I am put into?
I am still putting my efforts all for her selflessly and still incognito

She can't trust, is insecure, has issues
Why am I unnoticed?
My efforts in vain
Have I endured any less of a pain?

7. Writer's Grief

One fine morning, I woke up good
Washed up early, cooked good food
Got ready for a walk with my pet 'bright'
Can't make him bark and make neighbourhood freight
Returning home, humming a song
Was pleasant of a day where nothing went wrong
Watched T.V. soap till half-past two
Then began to wash my dirty shoe
A day so shiny, so bright
A bold loud sound of passing flight
What could go wrong? What could go bad?
I had absolutely no reason to be mad.
For, I recalled this dialogue then
You should be vigilant, everything's alright
I went in and thought to make some tea,
Was wondering the scene of the sea
The evening breeze inspired my pen
I hurried back to my writer's den
O god! My! My! What is it?
Running out of ideas, turning bleak
Tried but couldn't write a piece
Then I learnt what's writer's grief!

8. Survivor

The door opened, creaky sound
It was dullness & dark spread overall
A maiden in attire white
Down dragged veil in candlelight
Shadow pale from distance dim
She looked all gloomy as if committed sin
Suddenly appeared, abruptly vanished
All left calm but it was curtain
Wishy-washy she reappeared
Her appearance was so cold and murderous
Her head was down beneath the veil
Without a single sound
The friends on the table were high on the fourth round
She went past them and asked if they wanted more
Looking at a lady the whole hall roared
Masculine scent and inebriation smell
All teased her to open her veil
Neither did she oppose but she tells
"Don't be afraid, don't be mad
Once I open my veil everything will go fad"
No one paid a heed to her warning
She was considered ghost by most of them

When they were about to leave, she lifted her veil
She was an 'Acid attack survivor'.

9. The Real Iron Man

You fed us in the cold; you fed us in the warm
You fed us your blood & sweat, by working on the farm
You worked in the daylight, you guarded in the night
Such diligent labour worth my appetite
How am I supposed to pay for all your toil?
However, I strive can't be compared to what you've served
The blessings on my plate, every piece I bite
I am highly indebted to your struggle & plight
You worked in pain, struggled in the rain
Your endeavours served our appetite
The hunger pangs where we went mad
Your roti served a smile where all went sad
Your rice served right when things went wrong
Your sweat & blood became medicines & strides
The ultimate man, the superhero,
The real iron man, I call you
For, you fed us in the cold; you fed us in the warmth
You fed us your blood & sweat by working on the farm

10. Mother Nature

It is all in your mind
Cooked in your head
The feeling of malign
The young bloodshed
Terrorising world with unknown fear
Keeping distance from those who were once dear
Framing, alleging, taking the wrong path
Soon you will all suffer nature's wrath
Don't sow seeds of animosity
Rather try to live in harmony
Disarm your tongues of foul language
Let all together take a pledge
The youth will change the world's sight
The wrong will be eliminated by everything right
The boundaries can set us apart from each other
In fact, we are all children of the same mother
Nature did not raise us to see
The exploitation of humanity
Live and let live let the slogan be
Lets the world be a big family
Humongous enough to lend a hand of help
Not to fight, not to yelp

Be kind to earth you've been living on
Play in the courtyard of Mother Nature an innocent fawn.

11. Hope

Hope rising from the dust
Waning moon's crescent trust
Time will turn the course of luck
Untied the hardships struck
Pain will lead to the ultimate gain
Not a single effort will go in vain
Don't be furious, don't be shy
It's a matter of time you can also fly
The wings unravel the puzzle of time
The flight shall take off to cloud nine
Don't be shaken don't give up
Muster up the courage rise up
Beautiful is the world after devastation
Nevertheless it's the ultimate cessation
Wait for the gorgeous stars to shine
Everything will turn out fine
Waiting long will pay you well
In the words of history you will always dwell
Don't leave the string, delicate rope
For you have come across the adversities holding on to this hope

12. What If?

The world's most beautiful asset 'if'
The world's most beautiful heartbreaking regret 'if'
The melancholy of maiden 'if'
The sigh of relief 'if'
It's all about perception 'what if'
The maiden getting married deep in heart
Feelings of relinquish and becoming apart
Leaving her beloved embracing the new
The sole question in her head future's view
What if?
What if?
My family bid adieu me forever
Won't call me back or check me over
What if?
I won't be happy, won't be accepted right?
I won't be able to fit in their sight?
Will I have my mother's lap to return again?
Or will my parents turn their back on me then?
What if?
I fit in and settle down alright?
I would agree to compromise and lose all my might?
I will wear a smile every day

The best ever disguise
Will collect it every day and throw it in the bin?
The small fragment of my pride
Would be recognised as good but won't be a priority
Would be selfless and composed and be fulfilling duties
What if?
I be recognised by the world as a great potential
Will sought to chase mirage everything surreal?
Immersed in dreams will lose my loved ones
Or be a queen on the screen and off-screen a mere servant
What if?
I be treated 'Victoria' by my family?
In the name of a good, dutiful, cultured woman
Be never seated on the same table
Would I be able to hold my calm if I be treated dust?
Was it taught by mother?
'Endure my child –
As a girl you must'
The sociologists lose their knowledge
Philanthropists lose console
When the question of individuality
Deep lifted in my bones
On a skeletal full of praises, compromise and endurance
With my burial and cremation
The truth will always remain untold

13. Phoenix

A flight worth taking despite the danger
Fright exists, to overcome
Agile, graceful, nimble foot
In the midnight hoot
Left all the world behind migrate
Righteous, stubborn and fervent
Character had it all to be sharp
To measure all the world in map
I step foot forward to trust
The rest of the world with a beautiful burst
Of emotions, all bare all raw
Showing, making my childish flaw
Had it been bad if I was to bow?
Things went worse when I was clasped in claw
Soon became the talk of town
None the less a popular clown
Despite the bearing I had to survive
Then they trampled on my pride
I was burned to death and turned to ash
They had a fortune to encash
Misery did not startled them
Somehow I woke from bad dream

I saved the dying string of breadth
Deep in the veins valour bled
I rose from the ashes not to accept the demise
Can't let myself vanish can't let the death reprise
For I never let them trick again
I rose from ashes I am phoenix

14. Battles Won

The struggles we went through
The chances we lost
The opportunity that slipped away
It's all in the past
Our heads always held high
Whether in bliss or in pain
The experiences we gathered
Won't go in vain
We will rise from the dust
We will fight if we must
Won't dwell in the past
Will make the sweat shine
The worthiness of character
That's been polished and shone
After all, we've went through
Our glory will roar
The hands will always rise to support
No matter how bad they are hurt
In the labour of dusk and dawn
We will establish better earth
All lives together lost
Serious sickness & death

Humanity costs
It will suffer times again & recover
Leaving all calamities behind
Our tears won't be in vain
In remorse or in grief
It would be beautifully spent
To cast a future for the next
All the sufferings that we went through
Won't hold us back
As we are together
Adversities will never aghast
In the wake of a new world
A new era of oneness
The struggle far ahead will recall
The beauty and valour of us all

15. Be The Butterfly Of My Life

Be the Butterfly of My Life

Be the butterfly of my life
Nonchalantly innocent
No matter how you grow
Just be like how you always have been
I love your smiling face the most
Though I have sometimes made you cry
I like it all about you
Be the butterfly of my life
I can't bear to see you lose
Yet I can provide you to choose
You can have the entire world to explore
I won't ask for anything more
You go, you delve, you learn
I want to have the only trust of yours to earn
Be home when tired I will all await,
It's never too early or too late.
In the beauty of the shimmering world
Just do not forget where I dwell
Be back if it is late, be back if its night

You are the only world that's all I have
Be colourful, be nonchalantly innocent
Whatever you choose to remember,
Just, be the butterfly of my life.

16. Wrong Path

Having been lived a lifetime
Spent over self-justified acts of mine
No way to take a u-turn now
Amid this mess don't know how?
Walking on the shore, sand beneath
Is creating boil on bare feet
Is there a way back home?
Even if I return no one will concern
Since I called this upon myself
The whole luggage of miseries
I have been in the back a faulty fellow
Destroyed my family and all their mellow
Now that we have all forgot
Each other's address
I beg to choose not to differ
All this has been to me from the heavens to suffer
I didn't help my father's deathbed
Shameless how! I have no regret
When everybody was worried, took a wrong path
Was busy changing the world with my wrath,
The uneasy soul has gained some console
My mother is at the gate all assured

I have never played a hero, never played weak
For, I might be charged with, nature's stick
I am but the Lion in Den
Not a hero but a villain.

17. Earthen Fragrance

The feel of rainy days back home
Not on the border but in the den
A soldier's memories attached
A recollection of the earthen fragrance
His mother's culinary love during
The dripping wet droplets
The taste of tea in an earthen pot
The beloved memories of earthen fragrance
The game of football with his friends
During morning drizzle
In the park where it's wet
The recollection of earthen smell
It's been so long apart from them,
It's been so long being apart from them,
The enthusiasm, the vile, the charm are lost now
Our lion on the border is recollecting the past now
It's been days since he was home
It's been so long since he forgot
How it feels to be at ease
The only thing that can easily please
The eager scent the clouds release
Hopefulness dripping from the sky,

He holds the hope high,
He might not be able to make his way back again
At last, he recalls
The earthen fragrance back at home.

18. Morning Alarm

Snuggled up in cosily warm
Sweet and salty dreams of fairyland
Eyelids closed with innocent trust
Do fairies exist?
No, No, they must!
Playing aloud holding hand in hand
Under red little blanket
Silent and calm
May the sleep be cosy,
Little princess may rise up all rosy
Happy as always and full of charm
Snuggled up in cosily warm
Red little blanket
Silent and calm
La, La, Land full of beautiful beds
Little fairies, magic and charm
Sometimes the fairytale takes its bliss
The princess receives a true love's kiss
All giggling, making castle of sand
Singing and dancing, hand in hand
Little princess with big smile
Cosily sleeping all awhile

The dreams got broken by the sound
In midst of forest serene
There attacked a bee swarm
Ooh! I woke up its morning alarm

19. Shoes Of Colours

Shoes of all colours, Shoes of all class
Be it smaller or larger in size
Cute, Professional or feminine
It completes a look by creating a blast
It makes one Cinderella
It makes one Puss
It changes and supports persona
It helps to chase the dreams and run
Cinderella wore it
So did Puss
Both became magnificent
Characters among other ones
Shoes which are beautiful
Colourful and bright
And never leaves your side
They take the plight
They endure
All your emotions
Whether be memory delightful
Or broken heart

Printed by Libri Plureos GmbH in Hamburg, Germany